MY DOG

For Isabella

The author would like to thank Beth Aves for waves of enthusiastic design, Patrick Insole for the potato typography and Jackie di Stefano for the carrot photography.

First published 2002 by
Walker Books Ltd
87 Vauxhall Walk
London SE11 5HJ

This edition published 2007

10 9 8 7 6 5 4 3 2 1

To find out more about John Hegley visit
www.johnhegley.co.uk

Thanks to Methuen and André Deutsch Ltd for permission to reproduce previously published poems. Poems reproduced by permission of André Deutsch Ltd taken from GLAD TO WEAR GLASSES © John Hegley 1990

This book has been typeset in
Franklin Gothic & Kosmik

Printed in by Creative Print and Design, Wales

British Library Cataloguing in Publication Data:
a catalogue record for this book is available
from the British Library

ISBN 978-1-4063-1208-9

www.walkerbooks.co.uk

MY DOG IS A CARROT

A book of poems by John Hegley

WALKER BOOKS
AND SUBSIDIARIES
LONDON • BOSTON • SYDNEY • AUCKLAND

content

S

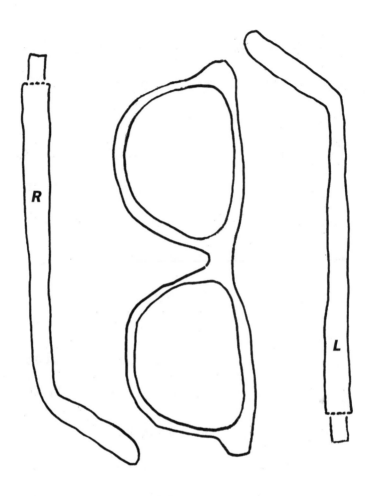

You can cut out these glasses and put them on: a) your face, b) your dog or c) your cornflakes

Me poem

me

me

me

me **ME**

me

Me me me

Me

me

me

me

Me

me

me

me

Me me me

Me me me me. ME me Me

Me

me

ME

me

me

ME me me me me

me me me me me me me,
that's enough about me.

my glasses are my glasses

Here are my glasses
they are brown
unless you turn
the colour down.

My glasses come in two main parts
the lenses and the frame
I really like my glasses
but they haven't got a name.

Well they have
but it's just glasses,
as simple as can be
I look after my spectacles
because they look after me.

I've got my glasses on my face
I've got my glasses in the proper place
but one day when I was running in a sack race
my glasses fell off onto the running track
and somebody behind me
deliberately hopped on top of them
and damaged them really badly.

Grandad's glasses

we never used to ask questions
about his glasses
he needed them to see the telly
and that was that
but then one day
he couldn't see the telly any more
so he didn't need his glasses
and there was no point in burying them with him
because
a) his eyes were shut
and b) none of us believed in telly after death
we had a family get together about it
and after the big argument
we came up with two possibilities
a) find someone with glasses like grandad's
and give them the glasses
and b) find someone with glasses like grandad's
and sell them the glasses

Grandma's glasses

my grandmother used to say
before you moan
about the muck on someone else's glasses
make sure you're not on about the muck on your own

her glasses were filthy

Wipe wipe wipe your glasses

I've seen people with mud on their glasses
I've seen people with blood on their glasses,
once I saw a lad
who had the leg of a daddy-long-legs on his glasses.
He thought they were cracked.
But they weren't.

Poem about losing

the place is unfamiliar
my face is bare
I've mislaid my glasses
I've looked in my glasses case
but they're not there
and I need my glasses
to find my glasses
but I'm going to be all right
I've got a spare pair

somewhere

My doggie don't wear glasses

my doggie don't wear glasses
so they're lying when they say
a dog looks like its owner
aren't they

A comparison of logs and dogs

both are very popular at Christmas

but it is not generally considered cruel

to abandon a log

and dogs are rarely used as fuel

loggie

Pet

John was feeling a bit lonely
so he decided to pretend that his portable telly
  was a little dog.
The screen was its face
the cable was its tail
and the screws at the back
they were its fleas.
John was very happy with his new friend
until one day she became very ill
after John had given her a bath.
When the repair man came
John called out IT'S ALL RIGHT PET
THE VET'S HERE!
and he led the man into the living-room
and showed him his portable telly all wrapped
  up in blankets
and the repair man took out a great big screwdriver
and pushed it into John's throat.
"Oh great," said John,
"You're going to get rid of her little fleas as well
  are you?"
The repair man thought he was teasing,
he didn't find it pleasing
and he took hold of John and he hit him
and the portable telly jumped up and bit him.

Max
(likes to be with people but people . . . .

Max is a dog with a problem
the sort of problem it's a job to ignore
the first time they all thought it was funny
but not any more
picture the scene this home-loving hound
is sleeping by the fire with the family round
he wakes up and makes a little sound
little Albert gets it first
he's nearest to the ground
Albert's mum gets wind of it
and she says open the door
and whatever we've been feeding him
I don't think we should give him no more
Max does another one like old kippers

wakes up Daddy in his fireside slippers
Daddy wakes up and says open the door
Albert says it's open Dad I did it when he did
   it before
then Mum says it's hard to relax with Max about
yesterday it happened while we were out in the car
and it's a small car
and Granny she was sick
she's not used to it like we are
maybe we should swap him for a budgerigar
Max is smelly
he can spoil your telly
but luckily
he's not an elephant

Volume, as in space

How many elephants
can you get in a car?
You can make an equation:
take the room inside the car
and divide it by the average volume of an elephant
and a more than average amount of persuasion

Books, as in libraries

My boyhood days
I spent the phase
in Luton by the Lea
and I always got a lovely vibe from Luton Libe-
    -raree
four new books a fortnight
it would to me lend
and as I turned the pages
they turned into my friends
the only ones I had
according to my dad

People
Using:
Borrowing
Learning
Internetting.
Closed
    Wednesday.

Local
Information,
Books,
Records
And
Relaxation.
Yo!

A BOY'S BEST GIFT

One day when I was seven or so

I told my dad of my desperate desire for a Christmas dog.

And he said "No no no no no no no no no **NO.**

NO!"

It didn't look too good.

"Why do you want a dog anyway?"

"Because I have no friends."

"But you've got Tony. Tony's your friend."

"Tony was my friend and then he got a dog,

now his dog's his friend."

"I'm sorry John, no dog and that's the end of it."

That Christmas my dad got me a kennel.

After the initial bewilderment

I crawled inside and became the very dog I had requested.

I became my own best friend.

RED POEM

Danger,

Don't tip that

strawberry jam

into the post-box

Stop, Stop! If the Post

Office van turns up now you'll be so

embarrassed,

Dad.

Pat and the

everything seemed flat to Pat

so she sat on her bike

and cycled round to see her Uncle Matt the wizard

even though her tyres were flat

and there was a blizzard

so what's the matter Pat said Matt

and Pat explained and Matt said Pat

let me look inside my hat

there's nothing there he looked and said

then put his hat back on his head

and went all red and rolled about

and spat a pair of glasses out

wizard

now look through these the wizard said

and Pat she put them on her head

and said

the world's NOT flat

Christopher Columbat

just wait until I tell my cat

she didn't know her cat was dead

splatted flat by Uncle Fred

it's lucky Uncle Matt was skilled

at mending cats his brother killed

and that's exactly what he did

and all he charged was fifty pence.

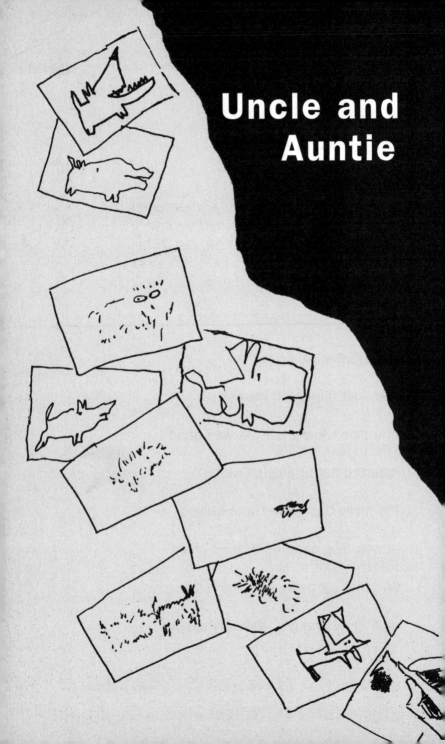

Uncle and
Auntie

my auntie gives me a colouring book and crayons
I begin to colour
after a while auntie leans over and says
you've gone over the lines
what do you think they're for
eh?
some kind of statement is it?
going to be a rebel are we?
your auntie gives you a lovely present
and you have to go and ruin it
I begin to cry
my uncle gives me a hanky and some blank paper
do some doggies of your own he says
I begin to colour
when I have done
he looks over
and says they are all very good
he is lying
only some of them are

Did I, Dad?

Dad,
Did I ever say how glad
I am to have you?
What about you, Mum?
No?
How dumb
How mad.

Mainly Pink Poem

Last
Christmas,
I got my brother-in-law
a pink jumper.
He was not happy.
When he'd torn open the wrappy
he said,
"I don't think pink is what a man should wear."
I said, "It's not off-the-shelf,
I knitted it myself,"
He said, "I don't care,
and I don't think men should knit
either, but that's up to you."
I said, "At least you can put it
in Thumper's basket."
(Thumper is the dog of my brother-in-law)
My brother-in-law said,
"Thumper won't sleep a wink
on a pink jumper.
He's a *boy* dog.
Pink is not for boy dogs, boy men, boy anythings."
I said, "What about boy ants?"
My brother-in-law said he wasn't sure about boy ants.
Then he opened the gift from my sister.
It was some women's pants.
Blue ones.

Sister, with this hand I made a fist and made it land upon your sandcastle. I am sorry. Let me make you a new one.

Poem About My Sister

My dad told my sister not to play with
  her food.
It was reasonable advice,
carrots do not make very good friends.

An owner's complaint

I've got a dog that's more
like a carrot than a dog.
It's hairy,
but only very slightly.
It's got no personality
to speak of,
no bark to bark of,
no head
no legs
no tail
and it's all
orange
and
crunchy.

For the soup

There once was an organic leek
that had managed to learn how to speak,
at the sight of a knife
it would fear for its life
and go **eeeeeeeeeeeeeeeeeeeeeek!**

Limberick

There was once a woman of Gwent
who was useless at pitching a tent
she hammered a peg
through a bone in her leg
and immediately after, she went
aaaaaaaaaaaargh.

The bare **BONES** of a poem

The skeleton gives flesh its shape
there isn't one inside a grape.
The skeleton is made of bone
it helps you stand up on your own.
The skeleton is strong and firm

there isn't one inside a worm.

Or a banana.

Or a potato.

Or a packet of biscuits.

Or a worm.

Oh no, I've said worm already.

Body poem

The human body's a machine,
the spaceship of the self,
and perfect working order means
you're in the best of health.
The brain is the computer,
the mind, a kind of screen,
the human body's a machine
that comes in many colours,
but not green.

Or anything stripy.

JEAN

Jean was keen on computer games
but not on hide and seek.
Jean lived in computer heaven
seven days a week.
She stayed in front of the screen until
she'd forgotten how to speak.

Bully for you

If you're being bullied,
tell.
Tell your parents
tell your guardians
tell your carers,
tell your home-sharers
tell your teacher
tell your headteacher
tell your deputy headteacher
tell the teacher who is deputy headteacher
when the headteacher is away
and the deputy has to move up one, as well,
tell all of them.

TELL

In class
by chance
I glance at her answer paper
protective of her labour
my next-door neighbour
drops an accusing karate chop
across the page-top
to stop me from copying
as she writes

her name

sub sobbing

The snub
at school I used to play a lot of Subbuteo
(a table football game)
and they used to call me Sub
and it was good to have a nickname
until they told me it stood for sub-standard

Jane and Wojtek

Wojtek was a Polish boy in my class
when I was about seven, Jane wasn't.
I fancied Jane, Jane fancied Wojtek:

**when I saw Jane and Wojtek kiss
I was jealous of their bliss
and I reported them to miss**

Listen

Mum and Dad, I'm feeling sad
let me tell you why,
there's a girl at school
I love up to the sky
but I don't know what she thinks.
I want to say she's elegant
and other words I cannot spell
but I just tell her
she stinks.
I want to be nice to her
but I'm horrible instead,
can I have some advice please,
and another slice of bread.

Breakfast poem

This morning I tipped
my cornflakes from the ripped
box, and a few flew onto the table.
Before placing them in the bowl
and spooning them into the usual hole
I drew them.
Of the drawings,
some looked like rocks
some looked like countries
none looked like pyjamas
and one looked a bit like a dog.
This morning I missed my bus.

What a poem's not

[X] A poem is not an **A**nt
but it can be quite short.

[X] A poem is not a **B**anana
but there may be something under its skin.

[X] A poem is not a **C**oat
but it may have some warmth in it.

[X] A poem is not a **D**og
and it can do without a basket.

[X] A poem is not an **E**ndless pair of trousers
but it can be quite long.

[X] A poem is not a **F**ootball
shaped like a cucumber.

[X] A poem is not a **G**oat shaped like
a piece of chewing-gum.

[X] A poem is not a **H**edgehog
but it might be hard to get hold of.

[X] A poem is not an **I**diot
but it can be quite stupid.

[X] A poem is not a **J**ack-in-the-box
but it can be quite stupid.

[X] A poem is not a **K**ite
but it might blow away.

[X] A poem is not a **L**ight bulb
but you can change it if you want to.

[X] A poem is not a **M**onkey
but it can be quite human.

X A poem is not a **N**ut
but you can give it to a monkey.

X A poem is not an **O**okookookookookook
ookookookooloombomanumakookoo.

X A poem is not a **P**rison
and it shouldn't feel like one either.

X A poem is not a **Q**uestion
actually it is sometimes.

X A poem is not a **R**adio
but you may have to tune in to it.

X A poem is not is a **S**cab
so don't pick it.

X A poem is not a **T**oothbrush
so don't clean your teeth with it.

X A poem is not an **U**mbrella
but it may give protection.

X A poem is not a **V**erruca
and I'm glad.

X A poem is not a **W**ig
but you can wear it if you want to.

X A poem is not an **X**-ray
make no bones about it.

X A poem is not a **Y**ear-old bag of vegetables
but it can smell quite strongly.

X A poem is not a **Z**ylophone
and it can spell words wrongly.

Loaf poem

I bought a loaf the other day
it came to life and ran away.
And I said,
"Naughty bad bread.
NAUGHTY."

L E A F poems

Let's
Eat
A
Fridge

Luton
Excel
At
Football

Lions'
Ears
Are
Few

Laughter
Eats
Away
Fear

Large
Elbows
Are
Fantastic

Look
Everyone
A
Fish

Tree poem

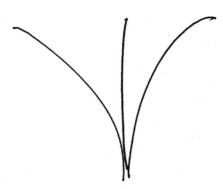

t h e
leaves
h a v e
all left
b u t
t h e
t r e e
will be
a l l
right

Key poem

Being a key
is my curse.
I live on a ring
in a purse
or a pocket
rarely seeing my true home.
Only for a moment,
when I unlock it.

Sea poem

The shallows
the deeps
the blues and
the greens,
the seaweed
and the submarines.
The lifetimes of swimming and no sweat
the yards of yachts
and lots and lots
and lots and lots and lots and lots and
        lots and lots and lots
of wet.

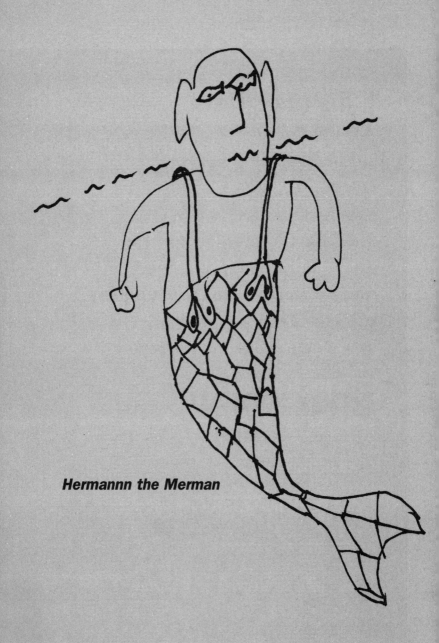

Hermannn the Merman

The emergensea

The octopus awoke one morning and wondered

  what rhyme it was.

Looking at his alarm-clocktopus

he saw that it had stopped

and it was time to stop having a rest

and get himself dressed.

On every octofoot

he put

an octosocktopus

but in his hurry, one foot got put

not into an octosocktopus

but into an electric plug socket

and the octopus got a nasty electric shocktopus

and had to call the octodoctopus

who couldn't get in

to give any help or medicine

because the door was loctopus.

The octopus couldn't move, being in a state of

octoshocktopus

so the octodoctopus bashed the door

to the floor

and the cure was as simple as could be:

a nice refreshing cup of

seawater.

∧ ∧

FLEA POEM

Dog's back.	Scratch.
Itch	itch
itch	paws
scratch	scratch
scratch	scratch
scratch	scratch
scratch	scratch
scratch	scratch
scratch	scratch
pause	
scratch	scratch
	scratch
itch	scratch scratch scratch
scratch	bald patch.

BEE POEM

I'm stripy and I'm wipey

when I'm visiting the flowers

I dust and dive,

my wings sing buzz

for hours

and ours

is a happy old hive.

I live in a colony.

I like to get all polleny.

Cup of tea poem

 Tea

 Tea

 Tea

 Tea

 Empty

Knee poem

Once when I was in a shopping centre
I banged my knee
and went,
"Aah m'knee m'knee!"
And someone gave me
some m'ney.

When the wind is up
you can get the height,
the   tail   flaps   wild
and the sails in flight
but, do remember to
hold on tight, otherwise you might lose your

BONFIRE NIGHT

the doors open
everyone comes out
everyone is ready
for fireworks
except the dog
Eddie
he is shut up in the sheddie
even out of doors they have indoor fireworks
Dad says it is better to be safe than dead
the air is full of the smell of next door's fireworks
Mum says they are very good this year
this year Christopher is allowed
to help his dad to light the fireworks
he is very excited
he is very proud
he is twenty-eight

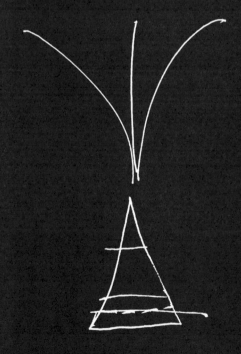

Armadillo

INSECTS

my mummy she bought me an armadillo
I kissed him and kept him under my pillow
and I cleaned him with a Brillo pad
he was shiny and tiny and he came from Peru
his name was Armadeus
but we used to call him Toby
he had a suit of armour and he burrowed about
the hills and the daffodils he turned them inside out
and my mother used to shout at him
when he came home covered in graffiti
he was an insectivorous creature
the teacher used to say
and the dog next door
the carnivore
would sometimes come and play
we had races and chases down by the willow
and sometimes we'd go swimming and sometimes
    we wouldn't
he had ants and beetles for dinner every day

them creepy-crawlies he could put 'em away
and he did his indoor doings
in his indoor doings tray
but one day in the winter
when the willow tree was bare
I looked under my pillow
and there was nobody there
I ran downstairs
and I said to my mummy
Mummy where's he gone?
she was having a game of rummy
and she looked up and she said John
go and put some clothing on
you're nearly twenty-four
and I said sorry Mum it's an emergency
and I ran out in the raw
and I ran down to the riverside
and in a rowing boat I saw
Toby
in the distance
with the dog next door

JACK iN the box

FOX iN the box

BEAR iN the chair

PAIN iN the neck

Neck

We used to have a teacher in our
school whom we called Neck.
We called him Neck because he had
such a long neck.
He also had big sprigs of hair
which came sprouting out of his nose,
but we weren't interested in those.
We were too keen on his neck,
we'd never seen such a neck,
it was a heck of a neck.

neck and neck

My dog is a dog

When I finally got a real dog of my own
of course I was glad
that I was no longer alone
but also, in the end it had
been good to be without such a friend,
as it made me see
the dog in a log
the dog in the telly,
in my jelly
in my cornflakes ...
and of course
in my carrots.
My new dog was great,
and he was worth his wait
in gold
and orange
and many other colours.

Goodbye